Chess
at St Andrews
28. 7. 2001

101 REFLECTIONS ON TAI CHI CHUAN

101
REFLECTIONS
on
TAI CHI
CHUAN

MICHAEL GILMAN

YMAA Publication Center
Boston, Mass. USA

Publisher's Cataloging-in-Publication

(Provided by Quality Books, Inc.)

Gilman, Michael.
    101 reflections on tai chi chuan / Michael
Gilman. — 1st ed.
      p. cm. — (Tai Chi Treasures)
      ISBN: 1-886969-86-8

    1. T'ai chi chuan. I. Title. II. Series
GV504.G55 2000   613.7'148
                                 QBI00-500077

YMAA Publication Center
Main Office:
   4354 Washington Street
   Roslindale, Massachusetts, 02131
   1-800-669-8892 • www.ymaa.com • ymaa@aol.com

Dedication

It is easy to recognize the True Master of Tai Chi Chuan. In this case she is young for her years, interested in all things, easily smiles, exhibits great love for all she comes in contact with, and has a kind and caring nature. She combines these qualities with incredible dedication to her art, an ability to move energy around in her body so that students can experience and believe, a mastery of the Form, and a precision in her teaching that benefits all.

Madame Gao Fu is a living, breathing example for all of us who are teachers and students of the internal arts that there are reasons to continue with dedicated practice, and that it is never too late to start. Gao Fu began studying Tai Chi seriously at the age of 55. Now, at age 83, she is really going strong.

This dedication is a small attempt to thank Gao Fu for all that she has given me. I wish that all of the readers of this book had the opportunity to spend time with this very special person. There is no substitute for being in the presence of and studying with a gifted teacher. If you have such an opportunity, do not hesitate to take full advantage.

Preface

The Master Key to attaining the highest levels of skill and enjoyment in the Internal Arts is intention. This book will help you clarify your intention. This is not a how-to book in the traditional sense. You will not find any instruction on how to do specific postures or forms from any of the Internal Arts, yet you will find general ideas and philosophical musings that apply to all aspects of the Arts, especially intention. It is more of a why-to book. If you are a student, a teacher, or are considering studying one of the Internal Arts (I classify any activity that is inner-directed, for instance Chi Kung, Tai Chi Chuan, Pa Kua Chuan, Hsing-I Chuan, Aikido, Judo, Ju-Jitsu, Yoga, Meditation, as internal arts), this will certainly help get you on the path and keep you on the path. In my three decades of studying and teaching Tai Chi, Chi Kung, Trager, Yoga, and other related studies, I have seen thousands of people start a class, and give up before they reach a point where they could reap the greatest benefits. It is disappointing for me, as these studies saved my life, and have helped millions world wide achieve greater levels of health and happiness. Sometimes it only takes one little idea, planted at just the right time, to stimulate one to continue. That is my intention.

This is a very strange time in American history. We are experiencing incredible growth and prosperity, yet our society is devoid of most of the fundamental conditions that contribute to health and happiness—family, security, trust, hope, and brotherly love. We seem to have lost the sense of future and the desire to plan on how to improve life for all. We have many billionaires, yet thousands, if not millions, of homeless. We have more people in jails then any other country. Obesity is at epidemic proportions. For all this I feel sad. Yet there is hope if we look in the right place.

Asia, and especially the Far East, also has been experiencing amazing growth. Some of the wealthiest countries on earth are in this part of the world. These countries—Japan, Taiwan, South Korea, China, Singapore—are some of the most crowded places, yet they are not suffering the same ills we are in the West. Violent crime is almost non-existent, education (as measured by standardized tests) is more effective, there is less difference between the wealthiest and the poorest, the cities are clean and relatively comfortable, and there is a sense of belonging and working to make the future a better place for all. What could possibly be the answer to this?

I believe that people in these countries have Confucius mostly to thank, for his gift of practical philosophy. His *Analects* are filled with advice that has been incorporated into everyday life, and it works. Confucius stressed that the individual is less important then the society; that harmony, truthfulness, education, and morality were of paramount importance. We in the West have our equivalent in the golden rule, yet for some reason, the Far East has maintained and strengthened these values, while we have, for the most part, put them aside.

The Internal Arts are based on the philosophy of Confucius, as well as on Daoism and Buddhism. That makes them special in terms of exercise and fitness, as they also offer lessons on living peacefully with other people in our society. Every time I practice Tai Chi, I am thinking about balance, beauty, tranquility, and many other principles that translate into a more peaceful and harmonious society. Many of our Western fitness programs separate us into individuals where competition is the motivating force.

I think we all know how to take care of ourselves. What we lack is willpower, intent, and commitment. As I grow older, I notice that even though I take good care of myself, I'm aging. I'm not as fast, flexible, or quick to mend as I once was. Yet I'm happier and healthier then I have ever been. I think a lot of that has to do with acceptance of what is, and having a life's work that brings me satisfaction and a sense of purpose.

Confucius said, "Shall I teach you what knowledge is? When you know a thing, to recognize that you know it, and when you do not know a thing, to recognize that you do not know it. That is knowledge."

This book is a sharing of the things that I have learned about internal energy over the course of my life. These are the things I know. I sincerely hope you will enjoy the lighthearted approach I have taken to present some important ideas. I feel learning should be fun and easy to understand. I guarantee that anyone who studies and practices the Internal Arts with determination in their hearts and minds will be healthier and happier. Please use this book to help motivate yourself through the hard times. It is not designed to be read through just once and put away. It is designed to be picked up frequently and randomly opened for inspiration. Please share these ideas with your friends and fellow practitioners.

As Confucius said in Chapter 1 of Book 1 of the *Analects*:

Isn't it a pleasure to use the things you have studied? Isn't it a pleasure to have an old friend visit from afar? Isn't it a sign of the superior person that he does not take offense when others fail to recognize his abilities?"

Nothing could bring me greater pleasure then to know you have read this book, thought about the ideas it contains, and enjoyed it.

1 Internal arts means the doing of actions with the focus on the inside of the body. We are concerned with how an action is done, not just the end product of an action. If I want to move from here to there, I do not focus on there. I look at how I am getting there, the feeling of movement from within. I don't think there is anything more fascinating then a body in motion, the coordination of millions of simultaneous events that come together in miracle like fashion. In a way it is like house wiring. When I turn on a light switch, a mini miracle happens— a light goes on. If we really think about how a light gets lit, we glimpse the workings of the universe. Universal *chi* is converted into electrical energy, this electrical energy is conveyed from its place of generation into my house, and then into an appliance, designed by some genius to convert electrical energy into light. Comparing our body to this house, if we want to move a finger, we have to go through all the same stages. Convert universal *chi* into a form of electric energy or human *chi*, then run it through

the intricate wiring of the body, conducting this energy to the finger muscles that will convert this electricity into movement. In the same way that we don't have to know any more than to flip a switch and get light, we don't have to think any more deeply then to just move our the finger. When it all works, that is. If the light doesn't work, you need more knowledge about the components and processes of electrification. In the same way, if you have a problem with your body, you need a deeper understanding of anatomy and physiology.

If you want to invent a new way to convert universal energy into light, you require an accomplished and expansive expertise, and if you want to grow more enlightened or self realized, you need to spend the time studying the internal environment of your Self. The Internal Arts are designed for this purpose.

2 *Funktionshust* is a German term for the pleasure taken in what one can do best. This pleasure — this happiness — may increase the tendency to do these things. This is nature's way of creating excellence.

From the first moment I started doing Tai Chi, I have regarded my practice as a

Menace

source of pleasure, and I have derived a great deal of pleasure from it. This made me want to do it more, which further increased my pleasure, on and on. An important part of the role of internal arts instructor is to help students find the aspects of the internal arts that they can do well, thereby increasing the tendency for them to continue their practice. For some it lies in the physical realm, for others in the mental, or the spiritual, or the restorative, or the philosophical. As instructors we must use our skills to look into the student, to help him or her find his special area of interest.

3 The Tai Chi Chuan form is much like a great novel in design. It starts out rather slowly, with an introduction of characters and place. At first this can seem plodding and slow and even confusing as one tries to sort out who is who and get a feel for the time and place and direction of the tale. Then comes the meat of the story. The slow and complex unveiling of the inner life of the characters and their interactions together. There are problems presented and the way these are resolved brings the real interest. Lastly comes the conclusion where all

the various elements and ideas are tied together and the reader is left with the feeling that somehow he or she is changed by what the author has written about. In the case of Tai Chi Chuan, the eight basic energies are the main characters, with *Peng* being the most essential of all. Without *Peng* there is no story. These characters are presented early in the form and are shown in their most basic self, standing alone. As the form develops, these energies become more complex and are placed in many varied combinations with other energies to make the form very interesting. On and on they move, one dissolving into another, sometimes very cleverly disguised, until the end is reached, and all is brought back to the beginning, simply and beautifully. The authors of these forms deserve the Nobel Prize for literature.

4 How beautiful and wondrous the varied styles and forms of Tai Chi! The current trend toward the standardization of Tai Chi forms for competition and ease of teaching is so limiting that I feel saddened. This practice takes so much that is special, and packages it for mass production. It is

analogous to taking a trip around the world, only to discover that everybody speaks English. The beauty of life is in the details, the variations. I get very excited to see other people's Yang style forms, how they go about interpreting the same material in different ways. I want to know how they arrived at their current form — did they consciously change it, or did their teacher? What is the cause for the difference between their performing a certain movement one way, and my form doing the same movement a different way? There is almost unlimited possible study in the history of Tai Chi, its evolution, its refinement, its adapting to the various localities and tastes of the people of various areas. In the Yang style, for example, there are differences between the northern and southern styles that reflect the climate and temperament of the people of that region. The north is colder, so people tend to move faster then people in the hotter south. The southern people tend to be more relaxed and consistent in their style, less prone to expressing the extremes that the northern styles do.

I simply love the idea that all the styles of today evolved out of one person's idea of what a martial art/exercise system should be and then spread to all the corners of the earth being modified by each and every great teacher.

5 Dr. Paul Brand, who wrote the truly excellent book called *Pain*, says osteoarthritis of the hip and its resulting pain occurs when the cartilage cushion separating the femur (upper leg bone) and hip socket wears down, narrowing until the bones almost touch. Sometimes they rub together, resulting in friction and severe pain. Now this is very important to think about. The ball (head of the femur) starts out as a smooth sphere. Most people tend to move legs in only one direction, straight ahead and back, as they walk, run, or sit. The bone scores along a single plane, resulting in some longitudinal grooving and the formation of tiny bumps and projections in the cartilage, which is the eventual source of arthritic pain. It is like forming ruts in a road from always driving on the same place. Once ruts are formed, it is difficult to get out of them. In my opinion, running and other repetitive sports that have limited movements only make this problem happen more quickly. I feel that Tai Chi and other internal arts are some of

the best exercises to ward off this almost inevitable problem. These types of exercise put minimal jarring and jolting into the hip socket, and use smooth, round movements in all directions, so no grooves are formed.

So do as many varied movements as possible, sit tailor-fashion on the floor whenever possible, and try not to form many ruts in your life.

6 I went over to visit a friend and she promptly sat me down in a comfortable chair and commenced to play me a piece of music on her piano that she was going to be performing that very night. As the melody reached out and enveloped me, my mind formed this comparative insight. My friend was playing from a piece of sheet music that had been composed by someone quite a while ago. She played each note as written, yet she brought to it all her life experiences—her intellect, her emotions, her longing. Each person who sits down to play those very same notes will sound different because it is their whole life that plays those notes. How like Tai Chi, I thought to myself. The forms were composed by people long ago in a far off land, and as each one of us plays the same forms, we bring all

our life experiences to it and it appears different then anyone else's. My friend's sheet music gives specific directions as to pace and timbre, the Tai Chi classics do the same for me. There are masters at composing music, like Mozart and Beethoven, and masters at interpreting these composers, like Glenn Gould and Van Cliburn. Tai Chi had its master composers like Yang, Wu, and Chen and master interpreters recognized by their contemporaries. So I thank my friend for her lovely music and the stimulus for thoughts and deeper appreciation of Tai Chi Chuan.

7 We in the West are not encouraged to plan for the future. We often hear the philosophy of living just for today, for there most probably won't be a tomorrow, because of the growing population, pollution, crime, dwindling agricultural land, and more. So people here don't take care of things, they don't take care of their health, family, or community. It is a sad state of affairs. Tai Chi Chuan is known to be one of the very best exercises for older people to maintain good health, yet here again, so few plan for the future. It takes many years of study to arrive at a place in one's Tai Chi

practice where it will do the most good, on the energetic level. One would have to start learning when they were younger to gain the benefits when they need it, yet it is precisely at that time that the younger person is living for today. This is a dilemma. Its never too late, but I encourage all people to start learning this fine art early, and not to stop practicing no matter how poorly you think you may be doing. It will almost guarantee a healthy, happy life.

8 Leonardo de Vinci was thought to say, "Start with what you can see, and learn from what you discover." That idea is important to me as a student and teacher. The form was given to me by a teacher. That is just the starting place for me to discover what the form contains, because a form is only that, a structure of something as distinguished from substance. It is easy, especially in the beginning, to view the form as the substance, and many people stop there. But with an explorer's heart, we can enjoy endless years of wandering around our internal arts, never knowing exactly what we will discover. It's the surprises that make life interesting.

9 The body and mind are interrelated and, at the core, one and the same. Both developed from one cell that was a combination of an egg and a sperm cell. It is convenient to talk about a human as composed of various elements, like muscles, bones, nerves, organs, etc.—yet, of course, it is all one. Let's look at the nervous system for a moment. The nerves are the link between the mind and the body. The nerves are the communication system of the body, and possibly the worst thing that can happen to a person is to have this communication system damaged, through for instance a stroke. All parts of the body are linked to the brain via nerves, and the main trunk line is the spinal column. The brain is constantly receiving messages from all over the body and tries to deal with as many messages as possible. When there are too many messages at the same time, the brain deals with the most important first. For instance, you see a gold ring lying in the street. The eyes send the message to the brain and the brain sends back the message to the legs to move and go get it. As you start, you hear a car approaching at a fast pace. The ears send the message to the brain and the brain says it is more important to get out of the

way of the car then to pick up the ring, so your body stops in mid step and you pull back. All of this requires strong nerve currents, good communication between nerves and muscles, and a healthy brain. All of these are trained daily through internal arts practice. The harmonious use of muscles results in harmonious use of nerves and a reduction of nervous tension. That reduction allows relaxation and calmness so important to our over all health.

10 One of the wisest persons I know of is a man by the name of Oscar Ichazo, who started a human potential group called Arica that was very active in the 1970s. He used everything that he thought worked from all spiritual and cultural traditions, and combined them into a truly effective system for helping people reach their potential. One of the exercises that I still teach and practice is a breathing, moving exercise with a very deep teaching connected to it. As one moved through simple movements, almost like Tai Chi, three words were chanted over and over. These words were (Oscar is from Chile so the words are in Spanish) : *Voluntad, Escuela, Silencio.* Translated, this is what they mean

to me. *Voluntad*= Willpower, *Escuela*= Teachings, *Silencio*= Quiet Mind. Putting it together, this means that with enough will power, correct teachings, and a quiet mind we can attain enlightenment. This sage advice relates perfectly to the study of the internal arts. You must have will power and intention to carry through with your study and practice no matter what. You must seek out the truth from all sources, no matter from where they spring. You must meditate and work with the mind until it can be quieted. If you take these three words and their meaning into your heart, you will reach your potential.

11 As the Classics state "if there is a problem with the form, look to the legs." The foundation of the legs are the feet, so let's look at bit at the feet and see if we can eliminate any potential problems in our forms. Dr. Bess Mensendieck really helped me to understand this dynamic. The long arch that extends from the heel to a point just before the big toe is best suited to carry the weight of the body. Several muscles determine this arch's shape. The arch may be considered as being supported by

two pillars. One pillar is the heel and, because it is fixed in place, we don't have to worry about it doing its job. The second pillar is the ball of the foot, the area around and including the big toe joint. The ball of the foot is made to serve as support for the weight by using the Peronaeus muscle. This muscle extends from the knee, along the outside of the lower leg, across the sole of the foot and is fastened near the ball of the foot. When being used, the Peronaeus muscle maintains the ball of the foot in place and thereby erects the second support for the arch. If this muscle is not used, the result may be falling arches or flat feet. By carrying the weight of the body toward the ball of the foot when standing or moving, you bring the Peronaeus muscle into use. In the internal arts we use the concept of screwing out the energy from hip to foot so as to activate this muscle. Distributing the weight between the heel and ball of the foot creates a reliable and elastic foundation for the body weight. So, if you place your hand on the outside of the lower leg and flex your foot arch you should feel this muscle come into play. Make sure you use it.

12 It is essential that the *chi* flows uninterruptedly through the body. This *chi* flow is often compared to a great river, and that is an apt metaphor. The river has many qualities that the internal artist wants to emulate in his or her own body including power, yielding, adaptability, and strength of purpose. Just as water hates dams, our bodies hate blocks, which in people are mostly constructed from tension. Riots used to be controlled by the use of bullets and now they are controlled by water cannons. Much more effective and less crude. The Tai Chi player uses the cruder movements such as punch or kick only as a last resort, preferring the skills of sticking, adhering, connecting and following. These have the qualities of water, being effective without causing harm. Take time to sit by a beautiful river and observe its flow and I'm sure your internal art practice will flourish.

13 Think a moment about yin and yang. What comes to your mind? Probably something about opposites, this and that. Up and down. Hot and cold, etc. But really, there is no such thing as yin and yang. I bet you're saying to yourself that I must be crazy to make such a statement, so here is my explanation. Yin and yang are only comparative words, words that describe something only in relation to something else. There is no absolute hot, or up, or hard, or maleness etc. When we say that male is yang it is only in relation to the female. And even that is not absolute as some males are more yin then some females. The idea of yin and yang is not to end up with vast lists of what is yin and what is yang for some unknown reason, but to help people find balance in their lives, and for no other reason. If you are too hot you need to find something to cool you down. If something is too concentrated (yin) you need to find some way to dilute (yang) it. The concept of yin and yang helps us to focus, think, reason, and explain natural phenomenon. What I'm suggesting is that there isn't yin and yang, only yin/yang. So we need to be careful when we assign an absolute term, like yin or yang to anything.

14 One of the essential points to all the internal arts is to lower our center of gravity in order to become more stable and to enable us to get under our partner, so as to cause him to lose balance. Hormones have something to do with this. Men pro-

duce androgen, which causes the bones of the shoulders and ribs to develop; whereas women produce estrogen, which stimulates fat to accumulate in the hips and thighs. Nature wants women to have lots of stored energy for rearing children and the best place to store extra weight is around the center of the body. Men were designed or have evolved into fighters and hunters, which required large muscles and the bones to support them in the upper body. Women naturally have a lower center of gravity, giving them advantages in judo and Tai Chi push hands, where low centers are most important.

15 Thich Nhat Hanh, in his lovely book *Peace is Every Step*, talks about consciousness existing on two levels: as seeds and manifestations of these seeds. Let me share this idea with you and how it applies to the internal arts. When we are born, we are like sterile ground, open and ready to receive the seeds that our parents and society plant in us. When our mother holds us in her arms, the seed of love is planted. If a parent slaps us out of frustration, the seed of fear is planted. Anger, joy, hope, disap-

pointment, etc., all have seeds and these seeds lie in us waiting for the right conditions to manifest. The beauty of this concept is that each time a seed is manifest, for instance if you feel happy, this seed becomes mature and produces more seeds of the same kind. So the more often you feel happy, the more seeds are produced, and the easier it is to feel happy again. The same can be said for joy, contentment, love etc. The more we manifest these seeds the more viable they are. If not used for long periods of time the seeds lose their potency. We all need to become farmers and sow the seeds for the emotions, feelings, and the way we want to live our lives. Every time I practice Tai Chi, I am planting seeds for health and well being, joy, hope, and expansion of awareness. These seeds keep producing more seeds until I am filled with them and there isn't room for the ones I don't want to harvest, like anger, hate, fear and selfishness. So stay aware of what kinds of seeds you are planting and weed out the ones that you don't want. We all contain the Garden of Eden and just need to keep it healthy.

16 The best way to deal with trouble is to prevent it before it starts. Each and every one of us can have a great influence on the lives of those around us. One can turn around the life of a troubled youth by being righteous and leading a life of truth and harmony. In 498 B.C., in the city of Chung-tu, a new Minister of Crime was appointed and crime vanished overnight because everyone idolized this person. The man was Confucius. So let's do our best to be good examples for all. The study of Tai Chi and other Internal Arts helps each of learn how to be a good role model.

17 The beauty of Tai Chi is that one can use it to express whatever ideas and philosophy one is living with or examining at the moment. After my first book appeared I received a letter and a book written by a women in Scotland by the name of Gerda Geddes. She had read my book and wanted to share her ideas with me. Her Tai Chi book looked at Tai Chi as an allegorical journey. She is a psychologist of the Reichian School, so that is her main model for contemplating Tai Chi. Her book, *Looking for the Golden Needle*, opened many doors for me, since I didn't have the keys for those sorts of doors from my past experience. I had never thought about the Tai Chi form as a journey for the soul. I tend to view the form as a vehicle for moving energy and as self-defense. I enjoyed her vision very much. It is very important to get together with others and share your views on a topic, even if others have much more or much less experience in the topic, as they just might never have looked at it in the same way you do. It also turned out that Gerda and I both had the same teacher, Master Choy. What a small and wonderful world.

18 The higher the skill, the simpler it is. This seems to contradict all we have ever learned, but think about this in relation to internal energy. Don't we want the thought and the action to be one? In martial arts, complexity usually leads to certain disaster, as complexity takes time and time is the most important element in gaining mastery over an opponent, (the other elements are power and technique). Reflexes are the fastest movements and the most simple. They don't have to be processed by the conscious mind. In Chi Kung we strive to allow the conscious mind to fall still, so that the

healing power of the universe can do its work. The more that we get our mind out of the way, the simpler the technique, and the easier it will be to hook up to the ultimate. Meditate on simplicity and you will be rewarded with certain success.

19 I have coined the phrase, "jumping onto a moving train" to explain an important principle of the internal arts—the correct way to join with incoming energy for neutralizing. Many hard style martial arts use strength to neutralize or block punches and strikes. Visualize the tight-fisted, right-angled block of the Karate practitioner. It is designed to break the bone of the incoming striking arm. It may be very effective, but it does not fit the philosophy of the Tai Chi player. We seek to join with, attach to, and understand energy as it enters our space. We seek to be as soft and relaxed as possible under the circumstances. So I coined this phrase, jumping onto a moving train, to explain our desire to softly join with the incoming energy. If you wanted to jump onto a moving train, you would not just stand in one place and try to jump on it as it passed you by. It is much easier to run alongside the train until you were going

about the same speed as the train and then hop onto it. It is similar neutralizing incoming strikes or pushes. If you try and "jump onto" (neutralize and stick) a partner's arm when it has gotten quite close to your body, it is difficult because the force has gained momentum and speed. The ideal is to join with him at the edge of your energy bubble (about a foot and a half from your body) before his strike gains momentum. Your body and intention will be moving in the same direction as his strike so you can join with him smoothly, softly, and without force.

20 Breathe as if your life depended on it! Think about this for a moment. We all know that our life depends on breathing, yet there is so much more to breathing then just allowing it to happen. In the same manner, there is so much more to life than just allowing to pass by unconsciously. Our lives can be meaningful and bring benefit to the rest of humanity if we have the energy to allow our greatness to come out. Genius comes from inspiration, and inspiration is half the equation for breathing—the other half being expiration. So take charge of your breath and you'll be

taking charge of your life. Breathe deeply and live deeply. Get rid of the old to make room for the new. Proper breathing will create space in your body and mind for the Universal energy to express itself through you.

21 We want to take a look at the Tai Chi body and compare it to the more traditional Western view of beauty and function. The Western ideal for a man is sometimes represented by Hercules. Huge powerful arms, chest, and shoulders. Tools to grab something or beat it into submission. The waist is small and very tight. Other aspects of this ideal incorporate a suppression of feelings or emotions, and shallow breathing, indicating emotions that are always right on the edge. The legs are usually not very important as most lifting and strength activities are done with the arms. The step is usually heavy as the body falls forward from step to step.

Now compare that to the Tai Chi body. It is heavier on the bottom, as most of the work is done with the legs. The waist is larger in relation to the upper body as the breathing and essential movement all originate in the waist area, allowing free expression of emotions. The muscles are softer on the outside with a firm core inside. The arms tend to have a sinewy quality. In the West we view the head as the center of control for the body, whereas in the East, the belly is the center. This difference makes for bodies and minds that relate to time and space in dissimilar ways. The West tends to reach out and grab for things it wants, while the East sits back and waits for the situation to evolve and come to it. The West is more like a tiger on the prowl while the East is more like a spider waiting in the web. Be aware that your body reflects your cultural, mental, and spiritual ideas. If you want to change your body, you'll probably have to change how you relate to the world.

22 The average person breathes about 700,000 cubic inches of air each day. In order to do this efficiently, many teachers of the internal arts, including me, stress normal abdominal breathing when doing forms. This is a breath in and out through the nose using the diaphragm (belly expands when inhaling, contracts when exhaling). There are other ways of breathing in order to accomplish different goals. To clean the body, the exhalation is

longer then the inhalation, and is through the mouth. To bring more energy and improve circulation, the inhalation is through the mouth and the exhalation is through the nose. The inhalation is longer then the exhalation. The Daoists say that reverse abdominal breathing can reverse the aging process. This is the opposite of normal abdominal breathing in that the belly contracts on the inhalation and expands on the exhalation. It takes a lot of practice to make this feel natural, and if not done correctly, it can cause harm. It is important to know what you want to accomplish with your body and mind. Keep your mind open and you will surely be able to find a breathing style to help you.

23 I think that most people don't care how long they live, as long as they can be healthy up to the end. We practice the internal arts to maintain a high level of health, and as far as I know, Tai Chi practitioners don't seem to live longer then average, yet they do seem to have more vitality throughout their lives. It's interesting that the average person in Roman times had a life expectancy of only 30 years, and that by the Middle Ages it had only increased to 40!

Can you imagine how differently you would live your life if you knew that you only had 30 or 40 years? At 30, I had just starting teaching Tai Chi and was very immature. At 40, I had just gotten married! The way my life is going I'll probably hit my stride in my 80's. We are lucky to be living right now, yet even so, don't waste your precious time.

24 Tai Chi Chuan developed in China over the course of thousands of years. First there were the mystical seeking exercises of the Daoists, who developed the idea that the body is the temple of the soul. If you wanted to liberate the spirit, you needed to have a healthy body, and it needed to be controlled by the higher self. Next came the Confucians, who added order and systems to the rather vague and more laid back ideas of the Daoists. Everything had to fit into an obvious order and if this order was followed, balance and harmony resulted. The Daoists remind me of the liberal Democrats and the Confucians are more like the Republicans. This was followed by the Buddhists who appealed to the needs of the time for people to look beyond this life, with all its problems, into a chance for a better life in the hereafter. There were no

rules, but there were systems to follow in order to achieve the final goal. I view the Buddhist path as more centered then either of the others. Tai Chi reflects all of these different philosophies; mysticism from the Daoists, order from the Confucians, and compassion and heart from the Buddhists. Every time we practice we reflect the beautiful, woven structure of the great philosophies of China.

25 Stress, especially unrelenting stress, plays havoc with all systems in the body. There is only one sure-fire way to deal with this as far as I can see. Soften and relax. Let me give you an example. Hold a pencil in your hands and slowly start to bend it. For a while the pencil will resist the force and nothing will happen. As the force increases, you will see the pencil start to bend as the fibers elongate to try and adapt. As you continue to increase the pressure, at some point, the pencil will snap and break. If we don't want the pencil to break we must either reduce the stress or strengthen the pencil. But strengthening the pencil will only work for a short time if the pressure continues to increase. Strength against strength always meets its match. The pencil

breaks because it is rigid, and unable to adapt beyond a certain point. If we really want to keep the pencil from breaking, we could make it out of rubber! Try breaking a rubber pencil (if such a thing exists). What I'm suggesting is to make our bodies and minds like rubber by relaxing and working on flexibility. The benefits of such training will pay big dividends, especially as we age, because that is the time when physical stressors really do us in. A fall when young means nothing, but for an older person, it can mean the end to a good life. Don't put it off.

26 Master Choy Kam-man, my main Tai Chi instructor, and most martial arts practitioners of his era used to go out into the streets and fight to see how they were doing in their practice, and enhance their reputation. This had been the custom for generations. Most of the people who study Tai Chi now do so for reasons other then self-defense. Yet we still need to take the lessons we learn in class out into the world and apply them. Can we help turn another person's anger or frustration into something he or she can look at and deal with, without lashing out ourselves? Can we join with another person and feel the direction of his or her energy, so that we can be useful as a tool in that other person's growth? Expand your goals out beyond yourself and look deeply into internal arts practice for help. Internal arts practitioners make wonderful councilors and social workers.

2 7 One of my students was having great difficulty with the idea of moving energy internally. She had thought that she had to trace the exact line or path of energy from the floor to her *Dan Tien*, and from there to her palm. Did this energy go up the inside or outside of the leg? From the *Dan Tien* did this energy go up the spine or on the sides of the body? Inside or outside of the arm? She was very confused. I teach the concept of "energy following the mind," so she was taking me literally. What I told her made her life infinitely more simple. Basically all you have to do is place your mind where you want the energy to exit or accumulate. If you want to push with the right palm, focus on the right palm. That's it. Very simple. If you want to do a left foot kick, think left foot. The energy will be there. That is not to say that meditative ben-

efit will not accrue from studying the body, meridians, theory, etc., but to gain mastery of internal energy movement one has only to pay attention to the final destination.

28 There will come a time, and I hope not too far in the future, when a person will be judged not by what he has, but by what he gives! There needs to be a shift in thinking about what is valued and important. As the 20th Century ends, teaching is among the worst paid and least respected of all professions. There is nothing as important as passing down knowledge and tradition from one generation to the next. In most ancient societies, the teacher, or wise elder, was a position of respect that had to be earned. If we are ever to get ahead, we need to build on the foundation of the past. We need to learn from our successes and our mistakes. Children are born pure and simple, yet lack all the qualities that maturity brings. I heartily encourage you to work to perfect your self, develop your unique skills and talents, and share these with any seeker regardless of his or her ability to pay you money.

29 When I first started teaching Tai Chi, I didn't think there was such a thing as a great female martial artist. In my classes with Master Choy there were many women who had a flair for doing the form, yet it always seemed to have a dance like quality, not martial. It was some years before I had my eyes opened by some incredible female students and teachers. At present, one of my heroes is an 83 year-old Master of Tai Chi Chuan and Chi Kung by the name of Madame Gao Fu. She really radiates energy and all who come in contact with her are warmed to the heart and soul. In 270 A.D. there was an Arab Bedouin women by the name of Zenobia, who defeated the greatest armies of the time; Roman, Persian, and Egyptian. She was not only a great tactician, but also had the power to lead and organize her people. She was said to have been one of the most beautiful women who ever lived. Sounds like an incredible person, and someone worth knowing. I'm happy to say I was wrong.

30 Master Choy Kam-man, always said "Respect Your Teacher." I agree with him completely and will even take this statement further. "View your teacher as a manifestation of the Divine energy." The Daoists viewed everything as divine, seeing the universal energy in rocks, water, air, plants and animals, as well as other people. If we can see our teacher as divine energy then his or her teachings will be the divine word and we will cherish them and honor them, and make our internal arts practice holy. I realize that there have been many instances of teachers taking advantage of their positions of trust and respect, so that we are now reluctant to allow ourselves to open fully and to recognize the divine in our teacher as well as other humans. Yet once you have found the right teacher, don't hold back. Your whole life will be enriched and you will be open to all sorts of possibilities that would not otherwise exist.

31 Progress in Tai Chi is hard to gauge. In most other martial arts there are levels of attainment as signified by belts. A black belt is said to have reached a higher level then a brown belt. In Tai Chi we have

no belts, so our progress is mostly an individualistic inner knowing, or if you are lucky enough to have a good teacher, the teacher can help you see how far you have come and how to move forward. I feel that there are three basic levels in Tai Chi training and these relate to the three Dan Tiens. The first level is the physical or martial correctness, and this corresponds to the lower *Dan Tien*. The body is moving according to the Tai Chi principles, and the student knows what he is doing. He has attained external control. The next level is integrating the internal and the external. There is a feeling of calmness and comfortable looseness to the form. The form is inwardly directed and the *chi* leads the movements as directed by the spirit. The principles are now in firm control of the external movements. This represents the middle *Dan Tien*. The highest level is that of spiritual attainment. The individual is functioning in accordance and harmony with the Dao. The spirit leads the movements directly without thought or obstruction. The individual radiates peace and good health, as well as the universal principles of brotherly love, concern for others, and a positive nature. He functions in the upper *Dan Tien*

with no fear of the next step. Once you have reached a level, you can function in that level or the one prior to it. You can even sometimes function at the higher level, but that is mostly hit and miss. I feel that the key to progress is practice and meditation. This will surely be your ladder if you only use it.

32 Handshaking got its start because two strangers would show their empty right hand (the usual hand to hold a weapon) and this evolved into touching hands as we do today in the West. In the East people are much more reserved, so they either hold up their right hand or press their own two hands together in front of their body (again displaying empty hands). The Indians press their two hands together in front of their hearts and say *Namaste* which means "I greet the God within you." The Japanese press their hands together and bow as a sign of respect. In Tai Chi we use a different hand greeting. We place the left open hand (left is yin or receptive, soft and yielding) on top of the right fist (right is yang or creative, firm, solid) in front of our middle *Dan Tien* (heart mind, emotional center) and stand tall and straight. What this all means is that I, like Tai Chi, am firm and solid on the inside and soft and yielding on the outside, am made up of both yin and yang qualities, and that my heart mind recognizes this in you also. I think it is a beautiful way to greet someone.

33 Water is the mother of all things, while fire is the father. Water is nourishing and supportive, and represents humility, as water always seeks to move toward the lowest level. Water is powerful in a very feminine way in that it is persistent and adaptable (water can cut diamonds). The internal arts owe much to water as we seek to move and change according to the obstacles placed in front of us. Tai Chi is sometimes called "swimming on land." I love the idea that water does not flow on until every indention is filled. On a physical/energetic level in Tai Chi we use a small amount of *Peng* energy to fill any sharp places, any angles, so that when we release the *chi*, it can flow unimpeded. Watch any good Tai Chi player move and it appears as if he or she is a roundish, elastic container, filled almost to the top with water, rolling on the ground. When it stops, it settles, and in movement it has enough give so it can adapt to the different shapes it encounters. Another wonderful property of water is that it can store energy in the form of heat and then release it over a long period of time. Whenever you encounter water, take a moment to pay your respects.

34 One of the skills of the internal artist is called wrapping. A perfect example of this is a spider as it wraps its live prey in a silk cocoon, or a snake that wraps its own body around the victim, both of which render the prey helpless. As an internal martial artist, I need to get in close to my opponent and wrap him up so he can't use strength to attack me. In my first Tai Chi Push Hands tournament, I was very surprised by the opening tactic used by most people. After making three circles in front of the body with both our hands joined together, my opponent would make a huge lunge and push in order to push me away which would earn him a point. I had never dealt with this problem before as I was used to studio push hands, which is much slower and uses subtle skills. I quickly learned that wrapping was the skill that would counteract this charge at the beginning. As the circles were ending I would imagine myself as

a snake and immediately let my hands tie up my opponent until I could slow down the action enough to deal with my opponent in the way I felt more comfortable. Use wrapping in different situations in order to slow down events until you can think about a solution more clearly. Wrapping and hugging are closely related; that could mean something.

35 The distinction between goals and desires isn't very clear, yet it seems important to me in my practice. Desires are a craving, longing, or wish for something. This strong feeling is something that can lead to trouble. Often one small desire can evolve into a very large one. I remember a movie of the 50's called *Quicksand* starring Mickey Rooney. He was working as a gas station attendant, needed $5 for a date, and borrowed it from the till, planning on paying it back on pay day. This small thing through a chain of circumstances eventually led to his character committing murder. Desires are like that. Most religions and philosophies preach a cessation of desire. I can honestly say that I don't have any desires at the moment. I do have goals though, like ending hunger, world peace, and education for all. Goals are ends or objectives toward which I direct my life. Goals have ends, desires are open ended. Self-realization can be a goal or desire and I think it depends upon the energy that goes into the thought. If I am trying to make myself better and reach the highest state possible, it seems ego directed and a desire. If I seek enlightenment so that I can help others and be of assistance to the earth and all upon it, I consider that a goal, not ego driven. So let us be clear about our goals and desires and eliminate the unnecessary elements from our lives so we can focus on what is really important for us and the rest of our beloved planet.

36 T. S. Eliot wrote in his poem *Little Gidding*, "We shall not cease from exploration/And the end of all our exploring/Will be to arrive where we started/And know the place for the first time." The Tai Chi form, as well as most internal arts forms, are designed to do just this. We start out with Commencement, which is designed to get the energy unified and directed toward the task at hand; that is toward inner exploration. The form then unfolds from simple to complex; from looking at one or two basic energy expressions to working with multiple paths with each hand and foot. We then head back towards simplicity and Conclusion. Commencement and Conclusion are basically the same movement, so we might say we have returned to the place we started, yet we are changed. Everything now seems clear, correct, clean and calm. I am always slightly surprised by how different I really do feel.

37 When I was in my 20's and 30's I did a lot of travel around the world, mostly looking for myself, thinking that the real me would show up better against an unfamiliar background. I guess that proved to be true to a limited extent. Now I explore the only real wilderness left, the inner wilderness of the imagination. The journey within is a lot cheaper and safer then a trip abroad, and is much more interesting. Just find a comfortable chair or sitting position, close your eyes, and let your imagination have its free rein. This can also be practiced lying on your back under a lovely shade tree on a warm day in summer. People used to call this day dreaming, which got it a negative connotation. Day dreaming or, as I call it, meditation on imagination, is a great way to open up and let the inner, real self come out in a way that will never get boring. Don't let other people bully you into thinking you are wasting your time. Just tell them you are meditating, and they'll think you are hard at work.

38 The concepts of stability and mobility are the foundation blocks of the internal arts. Stability implies something is resistant to change or maintains equilibrium. Mobility implies something that is easily moved. These are yin and yang, the opposites. Yang is fiery and explosive, always ready to affect change in the things in which it manifests, whereas yin is slow and deliberate, more resistant to change. Stability is more yin, mobility more yang. When we want to send energy out (yang), we need a firm and stable base to support (yin) this movement. When we throw a punch (yang) we need some internal energy to move downward (yin) to support this outward expansion. Visualize the strong base that holds the space shuttle in place for its take off. In the internal arts we need mobility to set up situations and avoid collisions with incoming forces. We need to move fast and be able to change instantly. Tai Chi

players generally can't move that well, as we usually play push hands with fixed step, or do our form which doesn't train quick stepping as much as stable stances. Aikido players are much more mobile, and need less stability even for their throws. Arts like Tae Kwon-Do are all about stability for their hard kicks, punches, and blocks. So no matter what art you practice, seek out those parts and movements that require you to work with the less used skills and make sure you understand how to utilize these abilities so you can be well rounded. You want to be mobile or stable depending on the situation.

39 Breath and tension are so very closely interrelated. I see examples of this all the time. I do body therapy, with the client lying on his or her back, on a table. There is one particular movement where I take the leg that is nearest to me, bend the knee towards the chest while holding on, then push the knee towards the table on the other side of the body. It is a good stretch for the hip, back, and torso. Virtually every time I do this, the client stops breathing! The body is under a great deal of tension so

the breath stops. I have to remind the client to breathe and then the tension eases some. I know the release of tension is complete when the breathing is normal. Now, take a moment and listen for the furthest sound you can hear. Do it now. What happened to your breath? If you don't remember, do it again. Almost everybody stops breathing and the body is in a state of tension as they try and listen (and be more quiet). When we concentrate, our breath naturally slows down or stops. In the internal arts, we must become more than natural, in that we want to breathe when under tension so that it doesn't have a chance to build. While intensely concentrating, we want to breathe smoothly, slowly, and calmly. The very best athletes almost always look relaxed even when under great pressure. Practice breathing exercises and watch your breath when under pressure. It may be difficult to remember at first, but if you continue a regular breathing practice, it will come more easily. In this way we can enhance our performance and learn to enjoy life's ever-present problems by seeing them as awareness exercises.

40 Lately I have been reading a history of the 20th Century, written by two Americans. What strikes me most is that, but for a few brief periods, our country has been constantly involved in war in some form. Millions of people have been killed for reasons too complex and contradictory to comprehend. As a teacher of Tai Chi Chuan, I must consider myself a martial artist, yet the idea of war is abhorrent to me. I see my job as helping people gain the skills and philosophical strength to move around conflict and into inter-action: a mutual exchange resulting in peaceful resolution. The stronger the individual gets, the less he has to fear his neighbor. The less fear, the more he is able to love and understand, which results in peace. We must use our internal arts training to strengthen our middle *Dan Tien*, our heart center, and let that energy express itself as compassion and understanding.

41 Would you like to help heal the world? How about those around you? How about yourself? It's simple. Just smile. You, like most people are rightly skeptical that smiling can help heal the world, but let me see if I can help you to see the reality in this idea. Please stay open-minded and you will experience the truth of this concept. Take a moment, sit up straight and feel how you feel, your mood or emotion. Do it now. Next, turn the corners of your mouth up slightly, a bit like a small smile, and see how you feel. Then relax for a moment. Next, turn the corners of your mouth down slightly, a bit like a pout, and see how you feel. Relax. Repeat this process; up, relax, down, relax. Did you feel any difference in the feelings that these movements produce? I have shared this exercise with thousands of people, and the vast majority say that they feel light, up, happy, bubbly, etc. when the corners of the month are turned up, and feel the opposite when they are turned down. The words they use are usually down, heavy, depressed, unhappy, etc. You see, it is only natural. When you are happy, up, etc., you smile, and the reverse is also true. That seems quite obvious. What isn't so obvious is that you can take charge of your own emotions, and this concept of corners of the mouth can help. If you start to feel a bit down and you don't want to, just turn the corners of the mouth up and you will feel better. You have now the skill to help heal yourself. Try another experiment. Next time you get an opportunity, smile at someone else. Believe me, they will smile back. Now you have helped to heal those around you, as they will also feel better by smiling. And as they meet others they might smile at them, so you have helped to heal the planet. Not a bad skill to have so close at hand. Smile. Besides, smiling saves energy. Smiling uses 13 muscles while frowning uses 50. Smile and you'll live longer.

42 Many people take great pleasure in practicing the internal arts. Pleasure is an interesting concept. We can say that pleasure is the opposite of pain; one encourages repeated action while the other discourages it. Pleasure is a condition induced by the enjoyment or anticipation of what is felt or viewed as good or desirable, while the opposite is true of pain. Pleasure, like pain, takes place in the mind and even more then pain is an interpretation of sensation only partly dependent on reports from the sense organs. I always encourage my students to look at strong body sensations as just that, sensations, and not to

quickly label them as pleasure or pain. If we view them as sensation it will allow us to move deeply into what is happening and experience the moment rather then moving automatically towards or away from a strong sensation. A slap can be an insult causing pain, or a signal of love from an intimate friend which we might find pleasurable. Let your mind be open to all experiences and enjoy being free from prejudice.

43 If we practice internal arts for self-discovery, we soon realize that our true self is hidden behind a mask. If we put in enough effort to strip away this mask, we will inevitably be faced with another mask, on and on, until most people just give up. Some of these masks are quite repulsive to us, and we quickly go about removing it, while others might be very attractive and we might think and hope that this is the final, one true self. These masks are the most difficult to take off as they bring us momentary pleasure, power, fame, skills, and even peace. That is why it is very important to have others around to help us, particularly wise teachers who have been down the same or similar paths. Let go of your attachment

to being who you would like to be, and spend your life discovering who you really are. At the core, we are all special in some way, and this real person is there for the finding.

44 As a general rule, body tissue flourishes with activity and atrophies with disuse. I remember breaking my wrist as a young boy, having it in a cast for some time, and when the cast came off, being amazed at how much that arm had shrunk in relation to the other. Astronauts lose bone density in space. This is certainly one of the main reasons for us to be practicing internal arts, since most of us in the developed countries aren't as active as those in so called under-developed countries. So do as much varied activity as you can, and remember that the brain is tissue also so it flourishes with activity just like the body.

45 Many, but not all, of the Internal Arts are martial arts: the study of how to defend the self without resorting to the use of excessive force. The greatest martial artists are those who do not have even to touch their opponent to cause a positive change in the situation. Just their presence is enough. Today, the martial artist fights battles on many different levels. I used to teach a Tai Chi class in a park. There was a particular group who hung out there, and who thought it very funny to come over and disrupt the "strange" activities of our class. Many were actually very belligerent. It took all my skills learned through practice to keep harmony, without resorting to anger, and without letting these individuals interrupt the class. I never failed, because first of all I felt love for these guys (it was always men), and wanted them to end up feeling better about themselves when they left. Even someone intent on causing trouble will respond to real love from the heart. So while many martial artists train muscles and body reflexes, I spend time working on my heart center, knowing I'm strengthening my ability to deal with unwanted situations.

46 I have several very beautiful rose bushes in my garden. The other day I was looking at one particularly lovely specimen and I had one of those powerful moments when one seemingly unrelated

thing leads to something else. On this rose bush there were many roses in various stages of opening, from tight bud to naked rose hip devoid of petals. Taking this all in, I had the thought that Internal Arts forms are like these roses — petals that open one at a time until the flower stands in all its glory. The beauty of the forms and the rose is not at only one specific moment, but in each and every stage in its growth from start to finish. Just as the fallen petals and the naked rose hip signal not an end but a feeding of possible futures, my ending a form is just compost for creating a beautiful life.

47 The perfect Tai Chi body would be a round circle with the arms and legs attached to the same point in the center of the circle. This may be hard to visualize, but I do think of my arms and legs coming from my center. When I step, my leg swings forward from my belly, and when I reach, that also comes from my belly. In this way the whole body is involved in a movement, and not just an isolated piece. If you visualize your arm as only attached to your shoulder joint, then it is easy to just do arm movements without using the rest of the

body, and that isn't acceptable in the internal arts. When I punch, I don't punch with my fist. I punch with my whole body and the fist is just the object that happens to be in contact with the opponent. Try this image the next time you practice and I'm sure you will be happy with the results.

48 Master Subramuniya, my first meditation teacher and guru, made the statement, "You can never be depressed if you can sit up straight." At first I didn't understand this idea and sort of poo-pooed it, yet I can say that I now fully agree with him. It fits in perfectly with the practical philosophy of the internal arts. We have the concept of *Jing, Chi, Shen,* with these energies more or less corresponding to the physical, emotional, and spiritual. *Jing* is heavy and sinks; *Chi* is neutral and blends going either up or down; and *Shen* is light and rises. When we feel unhappy, depressed, or down, our energy is low, and what energy we do have tends to move to our lowest energy centers to help us just survive. Notice the posture of someone who is depressed—bowed, head hanging, feet shuffling. When we feel good, happy, excited, up, our energy flows upward to the highest centers, open to creative ideas and cosmic thoughts. We are able to move outside ourselves. The posture of this person is erect, the step is bouncy. So what Master Subramuniya was saying is that by sitting up straight, you force the energy to move upward, and as energy moves upward you feel better. It is the same idea in the internal arts. We work with the idea of converting *Jing* to *Chi* and *Chi* to *Shen* so we can reach the highest levels of our art. Sit up straight, stand up straight, and you will be stimulating your energy to move upwards, thereby allowing you to function in your highest creative energy centers.

49 A glass that has nothing in it looks empty, yet it is full. Full of potential. That is true power—the power of emptiness turning into fullness. Fullness has nowhere to go but toward emptiness— yet even this is power, as any movement is a source of power. When I start a Tai Chi form, I stand like an empty glass waiting for the right moment to come to begin to fill. The first movement of my Tai Chi Chuan form is Commencement. The movement is

like starting with an empty glass, then filling it as full as possible, then emptying it again—only not all the way. I keep energy in my body from the waist down. Half empty, half full—ready to go either way. I can expand and fill into Ward Off or empty into Roll Back. This special moment is precious. Savor the moment with all its possibilities.

50 Yin and Yang, positive and negative are concepts very familiar to all of us in the internal arts. There has to be balance for you to remain healthy, yet in our modern society this balance is unique. Hans Selye, the psychophysical researcher who coined the concept of Type A and Type B personality, said that vengeance and bitterness are the emotional responses most likely to produce high stress levels. It is this high stress of our current lifestyle that causes most of the diseases and physical problems that cripple a majority of people. Gratitude is the single response most nourishing to health. Think how you can add this necessary ingredient to your everyday life.

51 We who practice the internal arts learn to listen to and trust the natural body. We train ourselves to accept a fall—to go with the wisdom of the body—not try and fight against the inevitable. When most people age they lose their sense of balance due to limited movement patterns and inactivity. When they fall, they stick out the arm to break the fall, which often results in broken bones and sprained wrists. This fear of falling causes a great deal of tension, which results in imbalance, which helps to keep this cycle going. Our internal arts practice contains falling exercises so we can keep the natural, rolling into a ball, response alive. With fewer corners, round objects don't get as damaged in a fall as sharp objects.

52 When doing any active exercise, the feet are constantly sending subtle messages to the brain. Most of these signals make it to the spinal cord and lower brain, but not to the thinking brain. Thank God for small favors. If our thinking mind had to control our balance and movements, we would never get anywhere. Watch a baby learn how to connect the leg muscles to the brain, or a person who has had a stroke relearn how to coordinate all the muscles necessary to get around. We take most of these body processes for granted. Let us give thanks regularly for this miracle of life and practice our arts with full attention so as to keep our body and mind in perfect working order.

53 *Man, man, man* is a mantra (a sacred word or phrase used to invoke the divine) often heard when learning Tai Chi and other internal arts. *Man* means slowly in Chinese. Slowly in this context does not mean slow like a snail. It is more like a tiger charging at full speed, captured on videotape, then played back in slow motion. *Man* allows the mind to fully engage the movements, feeling each and every turn as the energy winds its way from ground to hands. *Man* asks, "Why hurry. Savor the beauty, savor the miracle that is unfolding before your very eyes." If you hadn't eaten in a couple of days and were presented with all your favorite foods, would you gobble it down as fast as you could, or would you taste each bite, with special thanks for the opportunity to be able to enjoy this moment? Remember *Man, man, man* when you practice. You will be able to savor the divine.

54 Sensation and our perception of various sensations are important to internal arts practitioners. Yet it is interesting how our higher brain plays tricks with our perception. If I touch something hot and quickly withdraw from it, it feels as if I am consciously reacting to the heat. But the act of pulling back my hand was actually a reflex response organized by the spinal cord, which didn't even consult the conscious brain about the proper course of action. There was no time for delay. It takes fully half a second for my consciousness to sort through and interpret strong sensation messages, while the spinal cord can order a reflex response in a tenth of a second. So, for martial skill, we train until we can give more responsibility over to the spinal cord for movement response, saving the higher brain for more complex tasks.

55 Alan Watts was very instrumental in popularizing the Daoist and Zen Buddhist philosophies in the U.S. I used to listen to his radio program in the late 1960's and he had a big influence on my way of thinking. He said that the Daoist principle of opposites, expressed as yin and yang, pleasure and pain, life and death, "is more

like lovers wrestling then enemies fighting. The art of life is more like navigation than warfare." What a great way to express the idea of complimentary opposition contained in all events and actions. Many people drive themselves crazy because they can see that the results of their possible action can go in two different directions, so they become immobilized into not doing anything. We don't have to worry about making mistakes and getting off course in life. When sailing from one point to another, one spends much of the time off course, zigzagging across the straight line. We need to keep in mind that we can not fight against what is natural, only use our intention to help us navigate and flow in the appropriate direction.

56 I have often heard stories of martial arts practitioners who accomplish fantastic feats. The person who can throw someone far away with a touch. A person who can cause death with a touch, even delaying death for some days so as to conceal the cause of death. It is easy to disregard such stories as myth, yet it is so much more difficult to open our minds to other possibilities. If someone told me that you could leave your body and hover above it viewing it from afar, I would not believe it, yet it happened to me. If I heard stories about seeing energy coming off and out of the hand, flying across the room, crashing against the wall, causing cascades of color to rebound in all directions, I would tend to view such events as the product of a psychotic mind, yet it happened to me under and during a meditative state. These sorts of events only reinforce the possibilities that myth and reality are not separated by great distance. Open your mind to all new information, then filter this through your intuition, not your judging mind. Read the stories of the masters and be open to the possibility that these stories might be real.

57 The internal arts requires great receptivity of all the senses. The sense of touch is essential if we are to move to the highest levels of our art. This can be trained. Dr. Robert Fulford, a man I worked with in the early 70's, is the living manifestation of how an individual can develop sensitivity of touch. He is a cranial osteopath of the old school, who believes wholeheartedly in the power of touch as a source of healing. He has developed his sense of touch to such a high degree that he can put a single hair on a piece of paper, place a piece of paper on top of this and then be able to trace the hair under the paper. Try this and see how difficult this is. Not only that, he is able to place 18 pieces of paper on top and still trace the hair! Can you imagine how wonderful it would be for internal arts practitioners to be able to accomplish this feat? All it takes is intention and practice. We could all do such feats if we practice.

58 Most of us who practice the internal arts know about the concept of *jing, chi, shen*. These three energies correspond roughly to body, mind, and spirit. Many people are sensitive enough to feel these energies as they manifest in the body. People who mostly vibrate in the slower or *jing* range tend to be larger, slower, and like to do physical activities. Those whose energy vibrates somewhat faster in the *chi* range, tend to be more emotional, able to work with other people in helping ways, are more delicate in body structure. The people whose energy vibrate is in the *shen* range are the most intellectual and spiritual, tending to see events in the terms of cosmic rela-

tionships. They can deal with abstract ideas and do well with computers or arts. We are born with certain predispositions towards energy patterns, and there isn't much we can do to change this basic vibratory rate. It is best for our physical, mental, emotional, spiritual health to become aware of what our genetic makeup is and align ourselves with this energy. Be realistic about your expectations of your potential.

59 Everybody's life is an experiment in living. We try this, we try that. We take what works and cast off that which doesn't. The internal arts practitioner lives in a laboratory, constantly working with principles, movements, and ideas to see what works. To make a fine sword takes a long time of constant refinement. First the iron is dug from the ground, then it is smelted to get rid of non-essential elements. It is then shaped, folded and cooled, polished, heated and cooled numerous times to continue refining, until the desired end is reached. Our internal arts practice must be like this or we will never find new ideas, or better ways to accomplish our desired results. There is absolutely no reason why we cannot surpass the skills and abilities of the masters of old. We have the advantage of looking back on what they did and how they did it. We can take the best from all of them, refine these ideas with our own fire (will power and intention), and end up with a life that will be an example for all who follow. Don't give up on the constant refinement process.

60 There are three stages of sensation response in our bodies: signal, message, and response. First there is the signal, which could be any sensation perceived by our sense organs. Second comes the message, which is sent via nerves to the spinal cord and the base of the brain, where the message is sorted and either acted upon reflexively or sent to the brain for further processing. Finally, the higher brain (especially the cerebral cortex) sorts through the signals and decides on a response. How we respond or react is dependent on our personality, strength of sensation, training, and what else is happening at the time. Let's look at an example. You touch me with both hands on my forearm and start to push, more strongly with one hand than with the other. That is the signal. This message heads towards my brain, and since you are

pushing much stronger with one hand, that message is let through the spinal gate first and my brain then decides to move backwards and turn (a response it learned through training). Because all this is happening so quickly, the weaker signal of your light push with the other hand may not even make it to the higher brain, since it doesn't require a response. If we add other outside stimulations, say you shout and start to move your feet at the same time as you push, I might not even feel the push in my brain, as so much is taken up with trying to sort out these other strong sensations and my trying to figure out responses. The lesson in all of this for the internal artist is, when on offense, send as many strong signals as you can at the same time to over load your partners ability to sort out and respond.

61 As internal arts teachers, we must keep in mind that premature structure is detrimental to creativity. If we want to allow creativity, we must encourage free expression. So as a teacher, don't get overly concerned about form until the interest is kindled and the energy starts to flow in the area of internal studies. It is like trying to

teach a child to read before he has the desire or is ready. Once the desire is there, then one can start to impose structure, and even then we must be careful not to make this structure too rigid.

62 The term "centered" comes from the idea of centering clay on a potter's wheel. Only when the clay lies at the exact center of the wheel will the potter be able to form something from this lump of clay. When I was a kid, there was a piece of playground equipment that was quite similar to the potter's wheel. It was round, revolved rather easily in a smooth circle, and had bars to hold on to. If you were exactly in the center as the wheel spun, you had almost no feeling of revolving, but as you moved closer to the outside edge of the wheel, the centrifugal force would start to pull at your body until it seemed almost impossible to remain on unless you held on very tightly. All the internal arts work with this principle. If I am centered and you come at me with speed and force, I only need turn on my central axis to send you flying. The only requirements for this to work are that I remain rooted, centered and relaxed. Experiment with this concept by finding a

park that still has this piece of equipment, and get on the thing and play. You'll learn a valuable lesson and have fun at the same time. What more could you ask?

63 I read a poem by a man named Bernard Schlink and was immediately moved by a strong feeling that he could have been talking about internal arts partner practices. See what you think.

> *When we open ourselves—*
> *you yourself to me and*
> *I myself to you,*
> *when we submerge*
> *you into me and I into you*
> *when we vanish*
> *into me you and into you I*
> *Then*
> *am I me*
> *and you are you.*

64 The deep study of the internal arts requires contemplation on the body/mind/spirit. I find the body incredibly interesting. Take for instance, the fact that five trillion chemical processes occur each second in the brain, and it is from all this activity that we are somehow able to draw

meaning from the world. Or that a gram of brain tissue may contain as many as 400 billion synaptic junctions. The total in the human brain may exceed the number of stars in the universe. How utterly incredible. These sorts of facts, gleamed from my study of the human body and the internal environment, aid in my enjoyment of life and everything connected to it.

65 *Jukozo* is a beautiful Japanese term that means structural flexibility. It refers to the earthquake proof quality of a tall building. It is the ability of a structure to withstand stresses by flexing, moving with the forces, and not trying to fight against them. The internal artist knows this from the inside out. We never try and resist force by applying brute strength. That is not to say that we can't resist a certain amount of force with strength, but if we continue to practice in this way, we will never develop internal energy skills. Try not to fall in the trap of doing it the easy way. Have a partner push you, starting softly and working up until the push is at the edge of your abilities to deal with it. Notice your tendency towards using strength to overcome being pushed out of your center. Work at this fringe area until you can figure out how to apply *jukozo* to your body. You will grow in your abilities and feel good about yourself.

66 I love the idea that you can't get stuck in a round space. A square has corners, which allows energy to get trapped in them. But not so in a round space. Energy just keeps flowing. Near my house is an old underground reservoir that is huge and round. We go in there to sing, chant, and make music because the resulting echo is so amazing. Because of the shape, the sound just keeps moving round and round, creating wonderful opportunities for harmonies and layering of sounds. Nature does not tolerate sharp pointed, square anything. Energy has to flow and there is nothing that will withstand the ceaseless and never ending movement of nature's energy. Let us align ourselves with this energy flow by looking at nature around us, as well as within our bodies, eliminating any obstructions. This self-study will be well worth the effort.

67 Practice the internal arts and you will become smarter. Exercise increases growth hormones in the brain that stimulate the neurons to increase their size, and the number of their connections to other neurons. So as you learn new skills, you increase the number of neurons, which allows you to learn more skills. This is a never-ending process. Exercise helps in the cognitive areas of the brain, so by exercising we should be able to think, reason, perceive, and acquire knowledge more easily and more quickly. We should think twice about telling our kids to stay in their room and do their homework. We might gain more benefit by letting them go out and play more often. That is good advice for adults also.

68 One of the greatest acting teachers of all time, Stanislavsky, said "use everything in your life to create your art." I couldn't agree more, and I am sure he was talking about the internal arts. Life is so short, and if we want to move beyond the norm, we must use our time wisely. Every moment of every day is an opportunity to practice our internal arts. It is easy in the

classroom and much more difficult when under stress. Yet it is these difficult times that are the most beneficial to our mastery. Driving in traffic can help us with patience. Our dietary choices can make us natural. Relations with superiors and inferiors reflect our abilities to yield and lead. Growing a garden teaches us creation and destruction and the natural cycle of things. Do we want to overcome nature when we feel unwell, or do we study nature to figure things out? Each and every moment that we are alive is a miracle. We should take this incredible opportunity to practice living until we no longer need to practice, finding our art in every moment.

69 Stress is not always a negative thing. All exercise causes stress to the body. The result of our body's response to this stress is what we are seeking by doing exercise. Exercise is an intelligent approach to using this stress response to accomplish specific goals. If you want to build muscles, you might lift weights, because lifting weights causes the muscles to adapt to this weight by growing larger. If you want to play the piano, you must practice scales and do

other exercises to build the muscles in the fingers to cope with this added stress. We must use an intelligent approach to the correct amount of stress in our bodies. If we lift too much, we could tear the muscle (strain) or pull connecting tissue (sprain). So don't be afraid of stress. It could be your good friend.

70 It takes strength to overcome structure, and that is where technique play a part. If you set your body structure correctly, you will force your opponent to use strength against you. It is this use of strength that allows the Tai Chi philosophy and techniques to best be expressed: the hard is overcome by the soft, the impatient by the patient, the stiff by the flexible, the unyielding by the yielding.

Structural relaxation is a term I have made up to explain the idea of placing the body in proper alignment, so that the underlying structure (bones, connective tissue) will deal effectively with most of the stresses placed upon it. For example, proper postural alignment allows complete relaxation. If one leans in one direction or another, gravity will act upon the body in a negative way, causing the muscles to devote some of their energy to just maintaining balance. When playing push hands, if the structure is placed correctly, the partner's force will automatically be transferred to my root, actually making me more stable. This will either cause my partner to use more strength, making him clumsy, or he will start to move around trying to find an opening, which will make him vulnerable to counterattack from my strong, rooted structure. If I didn't have structural relaxation and alignment from the beginning, it would be me that would probably be fighting to remain in balance, and my partner would not have to commit his strength to his attack.

71 The hands are the fine tools of an internal arts practitioner. They have to be able to sense and convey to the brain the most subtle messages as well as, when needed, being able to concentrate and emit a most powerful force. There are up to 21,000 sensors of heat, pressure, and pain per square inch in the fingertips. One sixth of all the body's muscles are devoted to hand movements. A single hand movement can involve

as many as 50 muscles working together. Take a moment to look at the incredible objects you have attached to the ends of your arms and marvel at the wonder that you see. Take good care of these fine tools and they will serve you well all your life.

72 *Duei La* is Chinese for the concept of the movement of energy in opposite directions in order to bring balance and stability. If you move forward, there must be a corresponding movement of energy backward. Up and down, side to side, clockwise and counterclockwise, in and out. I live on the Puget Sound and often have to take ferries. One day as I watched the ferry pull into the dock, this principle was clearly demonstrated to me. A boat does not have a brake, so as the ferry approached the dock, it had to reverse its engines in order to slow it down. The faster the boat is going in its approach, the stronger the reverse drive must be to slow it. Seems so simple and yet when I push hands with people, there are very few who realize that they must be applying rearward thrust at the same time they are intending to push forward. This skill of knowing just how much rear thrust

to apply can only be learned through practice, just like the boat captain learns on the boat, not in the classroom. Play push hands often and think about this concept and you will have smooth sailing.

73 If you watch a cat in repose, you will see internal arts principles beautifully expressed. The body is completely relaxed, the breathing is slow and deep. Its eyes may be closed, yet there is at the core an underlying awareness. The ears move occasionally, scanning for any slight disturbance. The nose twitches now and then. If something unexpected happens, the cat jumps and runs in a flash. From complete repose to full movement in an instant. As we play our various internal arts it is beneficial to keep this image in our mind. Relaxed awareness that moves into fullness in an instant can be trained. Play push hands and games like that, and try to be that cat in repose. Touch your partner with the barest minimum needed to feel his center and relax. Wait for any disturbance then react. Perfect Tai Chi.

74 The only stance that is correct in Tai Chi, as well as other internal arts, is a natural, comfortable stance. If it is not natural and comfortable, you will lose relaxation, causing tension, which will result in loss of strength, speed, clarity of thought, and the ability to unify with the life force. In order to find a natural stance, one has to follow those who have gone before — your teacher and advanced students. Most students start with a shoulder-width stance, and as they get stronger and more relaxed, they move to a wider and deeper stance. This wide stance is not the end however. It is a training device to help the student gain strength, concentration, and internal energy control. When this wider stance is comfortable, only then can the student return to a natural stance, and have all the control he needs to gain mastery of internal arts. Start out shoulder width, develop good habits, then move to a wider stance, gain relaxation, then move back to a natural stance. You will be happy you took the time to follow this well-worn path.

75 There is strong admonition against bouncing at the end of a stretch. It is common knowledge that bouncing sets up a reflex that limits the muscles ability to stretch to the max. The body says " that's far enough, any more and it might be too much." This is true, yet most of the time I tell students to bounce at the end because we have a different goal in mind. Internal artists, when dealing with a partner, needs what I call dynamic flexibility. This is different than just stretching, in that we are equally concerned with stability; stability of the joints and connective tissue, when placed under tensions and pressures that change from moment to moment. You can over-stretch a muscle, and this can actually weaken the muscle and the ligaments that connect these muscles to the bones. The result of bounce stretching is a loss of extreme range of motion but a gain of stability in one's area of strength. If you practice bouncing when stretching, your body will be used to such stresses when unexpected pushes, pulls, twists, and the like happen when doing partner work.

76 Breath is one of the keys to energy movement, with intention being the master key. Martial arts practice uses these keys to increase strength, vitality, health and many other essential factors for a rich life. Chi Kung exercises are designed as general or specific depending on what you want to accomplish. The image of a bow and arrow can help with a very good, general tonic Chi Kung. The following exercise will be aid in experiencing both normal, and reverse abdominal breathing, both of which have a place in internal arts practice. Imagine you have a bow that is inside your body with one tip being the head and the other tip being the feet. First we will use normal abdominal breathing. The bow string is at the front of the body. As you inhale, the bow string is pulled away from the bow (belly expands) and as you exhale (belly contracts), the arrow is released into the back (*ming men* point). Do this until it feels comfortable and you don't have to think about it. Now we will do reverse abdominal breathing. Imagine the bow string is at the back. As you inhale the bow string is pulled toward the back so the back expands (the belly contracts), and as you exhale (belly expands, back contracts) the

arrow is sent to the front (*Dan Tien*). Breathe this way until it feels comfortable. Try not to force the breath nor use tension. The purpose of this exercise is first to experience both types of breathing, and secondly to learn to send energy (open communications) back and forth between the *Dan Tien* and *mingmen* point which is essential to reach the highest levels in internal arts practice. Try this exercise for a short while but with full attention and notice which style of breathing works best for you and if you are able to interchange styles at will.

77 *Jia chi bu dian*. This is one of the most ancient Chinese strategies in dealing with relationships, including fighting. It means to pretend to be stupid when one is smart. How contradictory to the way most Western people act—we try and appear smart when we are actually stupid. This doesn't necessarily mean to act stupid in everything, just certain areas. This strategy works very well in martial arts and push hands. When the opponent thinks you are weak in one area and attacks this place, he opens himself up to counterattack. Save this strategy for the perfect moment and you will be amazed at how effective it is.

78 As the teacher develops, so do the students; as the students develop, so does the teacher. When I first started teaching, I thought I knew it all. When I taught my first class and started getting questions, I realized I really didn't know very much at all. As they asked, I developed. I was forced to look within for answers, and as I went deeper, the students went deeper with me. As the years went by, I kept thinking that the students were getting smarter and asking more complex questions. The truth was that my knowledge and experience had grown to the place where I was teaching at a more profound level which caused the students to have to challenge themselves more and the questions that they did ask were more involved. It is a wonderful feedback loop and it continues to grow tighter and smaller as the years go by. A teacher lives for his students and grows because of them.

79 Every student of Tai Chi and other internal arts has heard the word "Relax" countless times. Each time I say this word I see students tense up slightly in trying to find relaxation in their body. We

have placed more tension in the mind by putting this pressure on the student. The Chinese say *Sung,* which has much the same meaning but is more of a dynamic state then relaxation implies. I have started to replace the word relaxation with two words—calm and comfortable. These words somehow do not cause as much anxiety in students and convey the feeling we are looking to achieve. These words let the student be who he is now and leaves room for improvement. Say these two words to yourself and see how you feel. They might work better then *Relax.*

80 Tai Chi and other internal arts have been demonstrated, in the laboratory, to produce endorphins. Endorphins, known as the brain opiate, have ounce for ounce, 10,000 times the painkilling power as morphine. The mind releases endorphins to dull pain, or induce feelings of happiness and pleasure. Time and time again I have demonstrated to myself, and have heard stories from my students and others, about starting Tai Chi practice with the pain of a bad back or sore muscle, only to realize after a short time that the pain has van-

ished. I know this is true, so by consistent practice, one can remain relatively pain free with joyous feelings inside.

81 In the martial arts, our first line of defense is our mind, a combination of what we call *Yi* or head mind and *Hsin* or heart mind. These two minds work together to produce the energy that we call our aura or external energy field. This energy field extends beyond our skin and the distance depends upon the amount of *chi* we have. When we are sick or depressed, our aura is almost non-existent. Our energy is required within to help us just carry on with the essential functions of living. When we are fully alive and "charged," our field can extend quite a distance, certainly a number of feet. When someone who is charged up enters a room, all can feel this energy, and conversely, when in the presence of a sick person, we feel a sucking of our energy towards the needy individual. So our minds, which control our energy, make up our first line of defense. The second line is our skin. The skin is such a miracle in that it is super-sensitive (like Dr. Fulford, we can feel a human hair under 18 pieces of paper) or super tough (normally it takes more then

500 pounds of pressure per square inch to penetrate the skin and cause injury). Yet a constant, unrelieved pressure as low as one pound per square inch can do damage. We can take full punches and not get harmed, yet a shoe that is a bit too tight can soon bring us to our knees, begging for relief. Take care of the little things, before they grow out of control. Constant worry is harder to deal with then an occasional crisis. Practice will strengthen your mind and body.

82 I think that one of the worst shortcomings of our minds is that we fail to see the really big problems because the forms in which they arise are right before our eyes. In our bodies, as in the environment, we wait until the problem gains momentum and strength before we act to stop it, and by that time the act of stopping this problem requires so much energy and ingenuity that we tend not to carry through with the possible solution, and therefor hope someone else will do it for us. How much easier it would have been to deal with the problem when it first appeared. Don't wait until the problem is already manifested in the body and then try and deal with it.

We work with the same idea in internal arts partner play. For example, if a car is parked on a steep hill, we could put a small block behind one tire and, letting off the brake, the car would stay. If you put the block a foot or so behind the tire and then let off the brake, the momentum of the car would surely cause the car to jump over the block and continue rolling. In Tai Chi push hands and self-defense, we reach out and contact the opponent in order to feel and listen to his body and energy. That way we can anticipate his force and direction of release before it has gained too much power for us to be able to deal with it in a relaxed fashion. If we daily examine our own body through the use of meditative, inner direct- ed exercise like Chi Kung, or Tai Chi, we will be placing the block right under our body's "tires" so any potential problems will be discovered before they get too strong.

83 Johann Sebastian Bach is certainly one of the musical geniuses of all time. His way of learning and studying can aid us in our study of the internal arts. If he heard music from a composer he was not familiar with and wanted to understand

what made this music interesting, he would write down the composition by hand and then rearrange it himself for other combinations of instruments. In this way he would be forced to really understand what the composer was trying to covey—the feelings, the moods, the ideas, and how he went about it. This is also how one can learn more in the internal arts. After having a solid foundation in one's own art, one can then study other people's forms and play with them until the essence of what that other form contains is understood from the inside. Just as Bach could not have done this without a solid knowledge of all aspects of music, you cannot learn much if you do not possess an in depth, working knowledge of the philosophy and basics of some particular art. Do not be in too much of a hurry to add information gleaned from others until you are well rooted in your own art or you'll probably find yourself very confused.

84 I had a dream the other night where I was playing push hands with a partner on the edge of a cliff with a dark, seemingly bottomless abyss at my back. I had no fear as we explored each other for possible weaknesses and openings. The play became

quite intense and all of a sudden I felt his entire commitment move into an attack. Time slowed as I easily moved my body out of the way. I held on to his left arm with my left hand, stepping back to my right, and his body moved right past mine and it was at this magic moment that time stood still. He was perched on the edge of the cliff, his left foot on the very edge, his right leg already over the edge. I held his left arm high over his head with my left hand, my right arm on the small of his back. His body was bent backward to try and counter—balance the inevitable outcome. It was a truly beautiful picture, which reminded me of a ballet. We looked into each other's eyes, deeply into each other souls, and saw the emergence of the energy that comes from accepting the inevitable. I let go of his hand and he sailed off into space. I woke up with a wonderful feeling of knowing that life contains very special moments and one never knows when or how they will arise.

85 One can increase one's enjoyment by viewing Tai Chi Chuan as theater for the imagination. The play is the form you are practicing. The author of my play is Yang Lu-chan and I am the director.

The main characters are the eight basic energies (*Peng, Lu, Ghee, An, Tsai, Lieh, Chou,* and *Kao*) with the five directions (Forward, Back, Look Left, Gaze Right, and Central Equilibrium) as a fine supporting cast. One's lines (movements) are to learned to the point where the actor feels the lines he says are real and spontaneous. There is even a little room for occasional improvisation. One of the beauties of this play is that we do not need sets. Any place will do, but a lovely natural setting helps set the mood. The loose, flowing costume of the Chinese peasant or martial artist is preferred by not essential. Raise the curtain and let the show begin!

86 Trees are beautiful and marvelous teachers if we care to listen. Trees can live thousands of years, producing countless leaves and fruits all to the purpose of continuing life on earth and not just their own. They make the mulch that enables other life to grow. I see my life like that in the respect that all the work that I do is directed toward enabling those who follow me to use what I have learned to further their own growth. I am so happy to see seeds that I have planted flourishing in many places. Teachers are like the mother tree with seedlings gathered about its base, ready to take over when the conditions arise.

87 I firmly believe that we are guardians of the earth with the cosmic mandate to make our bodies healthy, our hearts sensitive, our minds alert, our souls refined, and our spirits brilliant. The cosmos wants and needs us to help in its plan. We must develop to the utmost all our skills and abilities so will can fulfill this mandate. If you don't strive, but give in to disease and depression, you will not only harm yourself, but you will be failing your destiny. Always do your best, look for the best, hope for the best and that is what you will find. You will be helping the entire cosmos with your good work.

88 The body is a hydraulic system composed mostly of water. When I want to move weight I only need to think of my car's jack, and it helps me to stay relaxed. The jack is quite small, yet it can lift tremendous weight through the use of hydraulics. If I want to push or lift something, I place my feet in a comfortable, fairly wide stance as close to the object's base of support as I can. I bend my legs, place my hands on the surface of the object, either under or in front of it, then with my intention, I pump fluid into my legs. This causes my legs to straighten, and in so doing, causes the object to move. My intention is not placed on the object to be moved, or on my arms. My intention is placed on filling my legs, and as a result they straighten. So do not worry about not being strong enough to move heavy weights. Just keep the jack in mind.

89 The internal arts have always been used as a path to enlightenment, a path to the full knowing of ourselves. This path is not without its ups and downs, detours and obstacles. When we start on this path we keep in mind the final goal, and this goal is placed in the upper *Dan Tien*. This goal is of a spiritual nature, and our upper *Dan Tien* is concerned with spiritual endeavors. When we start out, our energy shifts to our lower *Dan Tien*, as this is our physical center and we will need all the physical strength possible to carry through the hard times. As we move along the path, we meet the obstacles, and this is

where the middle *Dan Tien*'s energy is called upon, for the heart's energy is concerned with love and understanding; all obstacles must first be approached with these qualities before the physical is applied. So if we decide to walk this life long path, we must develop all our energy centers, not just the upper *Dan Tien*.

90 Most students lose structural alignment when using *Lu* or Roll Back (withdrawing). They tend to run away. Against an opponent who is hard, this will often work. The opponent pushes with force and when the body is removed or revolved (like a swinging door), the opponent loses his balance. Against someone with Tai Chi or soft martial arts skills, this running away will only be followed by opponent's press, which will cause big problems. What we need to do when withdrawing is to seek out structural alignment the entire time we are moving back. With practice, we should be able to remain in control of the situation even when withdrawing. In the internal arts, we say there is really no such thing as a retreat, only a withdrawing to another strategic position.

91 Full contact fighting contests are quite popular right now. There are many lessons to be learned from these contests. The most important for me is that nice guys do finish first, and what counts is how you play the game, not just whether you win or lose. If someone can best his opponent without hurting him, he gains respect from all. It takes real skill to win one of those matches without destroying the other person, and very often it is not the big guy who wins. Technique is extremely important. If we can take a lesson from these contests and relate it to our interpersonal relationships we will have come a long way. We don't have to put other people down to move ahead. We don't have to hurt our loved ones when we argue. Martial arts training is not about fighting for most of us. It is about learning, practicing, and using the martial philosophy in our everyday lives to keep ourselves healthy and happy, aiding those around us to recognize their skills and abilities, and increasing our own enjoyment of life.

92 We probably don't want to give too much energy to the idea of healing the body through the internal arts. The word healing is backward looking, healing something from the past. I think we can replace this concept with the idea of working toward a goal or ideal. See yourself as whole and healthy and practice exercises that aid in achieving that goal. Let go of the past and put your energies on the here and now, and the path ahead. If you walk backwards you will only see where you have been. Turn around and enjoy the view of where you are going.

93 From the first moment of our lives, we are given boundaries. When we cry, the boundary may appear in the form of a bottle or pacifier. This boundary says stop crying. Maybe we were placed in a crib that limited our movement. All our lives boundaries were placed on our physical, mental, and spiritual selves. Many were there for good reason, yet they still had a limiting action. Breaking some respected boundaries can result in a torrent of new life. In the internal arts we closely examine each and every boundary and when we break out of one, we are then

faced with a world of new possibilities. Many teachers want us to mimic them and to just do as they do. With that boundary in front of us, we cannot possibly exceed the teacher's skill level. So use your will power to look beyond the words to the deeper meaning, and trust your intuition. Don't let anyone tell you that you can't do something. Break free.

94 The idea of balance is paramount to our success in the internal arts. It is so very apparent in the physical movements, and less so in the mind and spirit. Yet when we examine our lives, we see how balance is manifested even in our aging process. As a child, our body's energy moves up and out to explore our external environment, yet our mind is entirely centered and directed on developing the sense of me—the inside. As we age and approach the end of our life, the body's energy is returning inward, limited and small, self directed, while our mind flows outward, beyond the confines of our own Self, and is directed toward a feeling of unity with the life force. What a beautiful journey of natural balance within and without.

95 There is a saying, "A good teacher teaches what he has been taught. A wise teacher teaches what he has learned." I think that many of us in the internal arts have had teachers who have a good grasp of some form or system and can even share this information, yet rare indeed is the teacher whose life really reflects the years of practice and the internalization of the philosophy to become a true master. The same can be said of students. A good student mimics his teacher and can do as he was instructed. He feels confident and comfortable in the forms and may even do well in competition. Yet, he hasn't taken all this in and incorporated it into his life. A wise student studies the why as well as the how. He finds the philosophy in everything he sees and does and applies the lessons to all aspects of his life. He has no goal in mind, only a love for the journey.

96 Do-Re-Mi-Fa-Sol-La-Ti-Do. From those few notes, all the songs we sing are constructed. Eight basic sounds, or since sound is nothing but waves of energy, we can say eight basic energies create an infinite number of possibilities. In the

Chinese Internal Arts we also have eight basic energies—*peng* (ward-off), *lu* (roll back), *ghee* (press), *an* (push), *tsai* (pull down), *lieh* (split), *chou* (elbow), and *kao* (shoulder)—that make up all the hundreds of movements in Tai Chi Chuan. There are eight trigrams that surround the Tai Chi symbol to signify the Pa Kua, another internal art of China. These same eight trigrams are combined into 64 hexagrams to make up the *I-Ching*, which is the oldest known book of philosophy from China. So we should not get hung up in the idea of how complex the internal arts are, but look at how very simple the basic structure really is. Concentrate on these eight basic energies and all the variations in the form will be simple.

97 Dogs and cats can teach us a great deal about martial skill and interpersonal relations if we take the time to observe. I like animals and always make an effort to interact with them. Let's say I meet a strange cat and reach out to pet it. Being a cautious creature, the cat may allow me to come close, but as my hand gets near to its body, it will gently and easily move just the

one place I am about to touch, out of the way. It will only allow me so close but tease me into thinking it wants to be petted by not moving its whole body away. A shy dog, on the other hand, might not even let me get near. It will move away and keep a certain distance. The cat's skill is very high to allow me to get so close and then just move the slightest bit to keep me from touching it. When playing push hands, think about the cat, not the dog. Do not run away, but stay close and only move away the part of the body that is under attack.

98 Socrates had a prayer that went "Grant that the inner and the outer man can be as one." He obviously was talking about internal arts practitioners. Rare are those moments when our bodies move as directed by our mind, and our minds move as directed by our spirit. Rarer still is when the spirit moves the body directly. Work for and cherish those special moments when you don't have to think about what you do, yet it is done with full consciousness and attention.

99 Every effective force issued from our body is met with an equal and opposite force. As we push forward, our back foot pushes us forward and our forward foot acts as a brake by pushing upward and back. If the hands are pushing straight ahead, the center of the back pushes backwards. If we push downward, the top of the head pushes up. When kicking, the kicking foot moves outward while the standing foot is pushed down. It sounds so complicated, yet this is just the natural way that the body deals with such activities. In Tai Chi and other internal arts, we break movements down until they seem very unnatural in order to understand the dynamics involved, then we put them back together in a natural way, with the possibility that we may have corrected any unnatural elements that might have been present before we started our exploration.

100 Patience is a Tai Chi player's best friend. There is pressure to take control of a situation, even before it has matured. It is like picking fruit before it is ripe. When playing push hands, sparring, or free fighting, you must have patience and wait for the opponent to make the first move. As he comes out of his defensive position he is much more open to being controlled. And it is control that we are seeking, certainly not harm. To control our opponent without doing harm breeds respect, not hate and feelings of revenge. So wait and do the very least you need to do to gain control of the situation and all will be better off.

101 Internal artists prepare daily for their death. We do not welcome nor hope for death, yet we prepare, and we do it in the same way we prepare for any encounter—with knowledge and trust. Internal artists spend most of their training time learning about themselves, their body, mind, and spirit, and translate this self inquiry into practical day to day applications. This training brings confidence, and with confidence comes the ability to trust. For death we must train and learn from the elders, the wise ones, and traditional teachings. There are even some that have died and returned to tell of their experiences. Elizabeth Kubler Ross wrote an excellent book about this topic, *On Death and Dying*.

One of my dear friends, a poet, saw his death approaching and he made it his work, his gift to others. He kept a close eye on his feelings and emotions, as well as his physical transformation, and he wrote about it. He left his body with a smile on his face, and the name of God on his lips. His love enabled him to trust and this brought confidence that all would be well, and why not? So, daily I train and prepare by doing my best, keeping my heart and mind open, and trusting that there is some reason for me to be here, and a correct time for me to leave. I thank my dear friend for his guidance.

About the Author

Michael Gilman, a long-time teacher in the human potential movement, was born in San Francisco in 1943. After graduating from the University of Arizona with a degree in Theater Arts, he worked as a television director, actor, and dancer.

Gilman began his studies of Tai Chi Chuan in 1968 with Master Choy Kam-man in San Francisco. Master Choy's father Choy Hok-peng, a long-time student of Yang Cheng Fu, is credited with introducing,Tai Chi to America in the 1940s. Master Choy taught the full Yang Style curriculum and that is the system that Michael still practices and teaches.

Michael was authorized to teach by Master Choy in 1973 and moved to Tucson, Arizona to begin teaching. Over the next eight years Michael worked with over a thousand people, including such diverse groups as the Tucson Ballet Co., Tucson Opera, Tucson Museum of Art, University of Arizona, Tucson Public Schools, YMCA, as well as running a successful Tai Chi Studio.

During this period he also taught in Florida, Oregon, California, and New Zealand.

In 1981, Michael moved to Port Townsend, Washington and opened his Studio where he continues to lead classes and workshops. Besides his long-term association with Master Choy, Michael has studied with Jou Tsung Hwa, Dr. Yang Jwing-Ming, T.Y. Peng, T.T. Liang, George Xu, William Chen, Liang Shou-Yu, Tao Ping-Siang, Fu Shen Yuan, Gao Fu, Ken Cohen, and Sam Masich.

In 1994, Michael won the title of Grand Champion at the prestigious "Taste of China" All Tai Chi Tournament in Virginia. In 1995, he was honored by being chosen as an Advanced Form Judge of Internal Arts at the International Kung Fu Championships in Seattle.

Michael published *A String of Pearls*. Now in its second edition (the title was changed to *108 Insights into Tai Chi Chuan*), it has proven to be a very popular book for all people interested in the Internal Arts and Self-Improvement. He has also published many articles in *Tai Chi Magazine*, produced various video tapes, and written *The Tai Chi Manual*, a study guide for students and teachers of the Yang Style of Tai Chi. Michael has also been much honored for his continued dedication to helping teenagers.

Michael's eclectic interests, studies, and teaching include Advita Yoga with Master Subramuniya (Michael was his personal chef), Hatha Yoga with Swami Vishnudevananda (Michael taught Hatha Yoga at the Vishnudevananda Ashram), Zen Buddhism, Arica (Michael taught Arica in Tucson), Trager Psychophysical Integration

(Michael taught for the Trager Institute), and Dependable Strengths (Michael teaches for the Dependable Strengths Institute).

For the last several years Michael has been developing, a unique system integrating many of his previous studies.

It is called **Opening The Gates Chi Kung**. It is a synthesis of Tai Chi movements, Chi Kung, Yoga, strength, exercises, and meditations with the purpose of opening the body to the natural flow of energy. He is currently training teachers at his studio in Port Townsend.

Michael also organizes the annual **Energetic Retreat at Lake Crescent** in the Olympic National Park on Labor Day weekend which brings together teachers and students from around the world.